About this Book

If you're unsure whether to include a Preface, a Foreword, or a Prologue in your book, or don't know what an Epigraph or a Colophon are, *The Publisher's Guide to Book Anatomy* is for you.

If you're an independent author publishing your own book, success depends on learning as much about publishing, book design, and marketing as about writing. This reference to Book Anatomy bridges part of that knowledge gap.

If you're an established publishing house, this manual will serve as a useful reference for your editors, authors, and designers.

This book is ordered differently than a traditional book. The "inner" book pages—including a simulated cover—illustrate the various types of content. Descriptive "outer" pages (like this one) explain each element of Book Anatomy, including how and when to use it.

The Publisher's Guide to
BOOK ANATOMY

DAVE BRICKER

ESSENTIAL ABSURDITIES PRESS

This book may not be reproduced, transmitted, or stored in whole or in part by any means, including graphic, electronic, or mechanical without the express written consent of the publisher except in the case of brief quotations embodied in critical articles and reviews.

Cover and book design by Dave Bricker.
ISBN: 978-0-9862960-1-7

© 2018
ESSENTIAL ABSURDITIES PRESS
Miami, FL

http://www.theworldsgreatestbook.com

printed in USA

Table of Contents

Section I Front Matter

Section II Book Matter

Section III Back Matter

Table of Contents (continued)

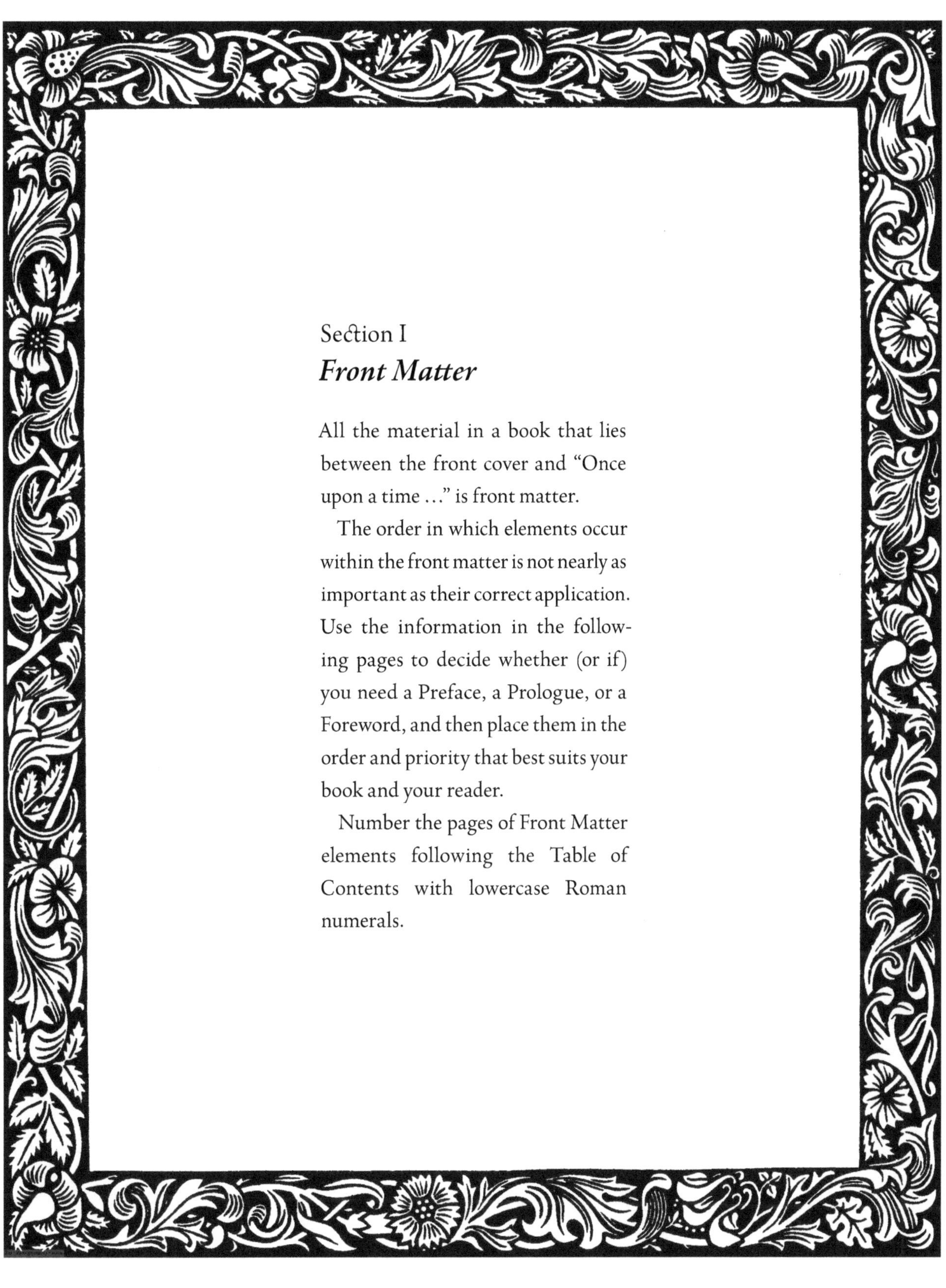

Section I

Front Matter

All the material in a book that lies between the front cover and "Once upon a time …" is front matter.

The order in which elements occur within the front matter is not nearly as important as their correct application. Use the information in the following pages to decide whether (or if) you need a Preface, a Prologue, or a Foreword, and then place them in the order and priority that best suits your book and your reader.

Number the pages of Front Matter elements following the Table of Contents with lowercase Roman numerals.

The Publisher's
Guide to
BOOK
ANATOMY
by Dave Bricker

Border adapted from *The Manual of Linotype Typography*

Front Cover

Book cover design is a subject unto itself, but your book *will* be judged by its cover.

If possible, engage a professional designer who understands book layout and typography—ideally one who has read your book.

Just as too many authors publish without bothering to learn about the publishing business, too many create their own covers without learning about design.

Crowdsourcing appeals to many, but if you lack the training to create an engaging cover on your own, you may lack the perspective to judge a design contest. When possible, engage a professional designer to read your book and create a cover that's as compelling as your narrative.

Don't assume covers found in bookstores are well-designed just because they have big publishers' imprints on them. Many are not worth imitating.

Whether you hire a designer or fly solo, buy a book on cover design to inform your ideas and conversations. Share your concepts with book design communities on social media where you can ask for guidance and critique.

Inside Front Cover

In books produced through contemporary mass production this "page" is traditionally left blank; the book binding process usually requires it to be so, though some printers do offer "duplex" covers.

Antique books were often bound with fanciful "end papers" as depicted in this example.

Other uses for the inside front cover include affixing an envelope for the book's library card, or a book plate identifying the owner.

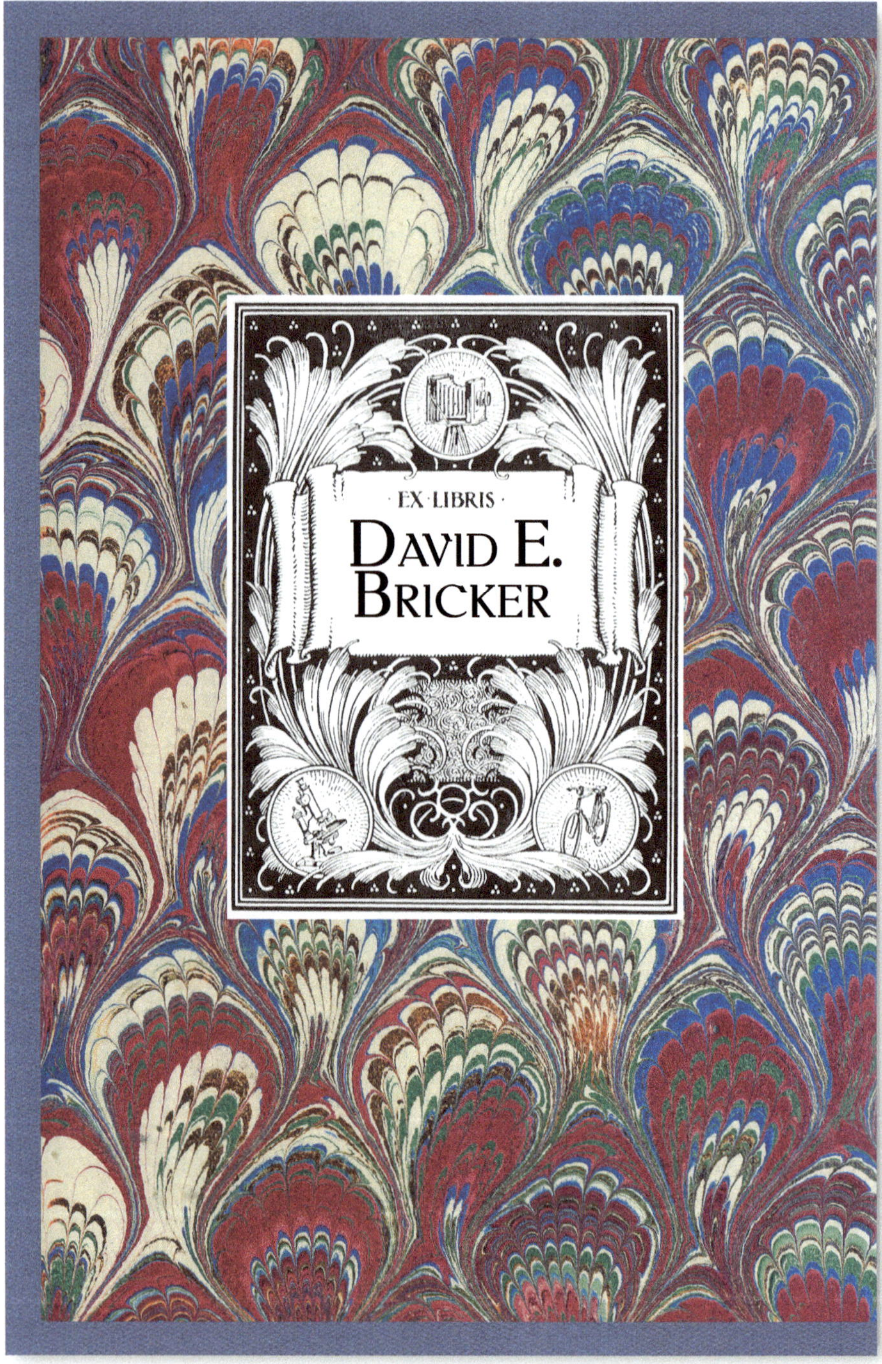

Book Plate - http://www.papergreat.com/2012/01/herbert-w-rhodes-early-20th-century.html

Praise for *The Publisher's Guide to Book Anatomy*

Place this book next to your dictionary, your thesaurus, and your style manual. *The Publisher's Guide to Book Anatomy* is the missing volume in your publishing reference library.

—Dr. Margarita Gurri, Ph.D, CSP

Lovely to look at and quite clear, *The Publisher's Guide to Book Anatomy* is a supremely useful book that will likely become a part of the universal canon for those publishing on their own.

—William Scott Miller, MFA
Dean, Academic Affairs, Broward College

This is a book not just for anyone who wants to publish a book but for anyone who loves books and wants to know more about what goes into holding something precious in your hands.

—Steven Bauer, Editor

Though this book is not about book design per se, a traditional grid of ninths is used for page layout. On pages where the content does not fill the text area (like this one), the content is centered and appropriate guides are shown. See Page Layout: Illustrated Books and the Rule of Thirds http://theworldsgreatestbook.com/page-layout-rule-of-thirds/

Praise for the Book

A few quotes from advance reviews are sometimes placed immediately inside the front cover on unnumbered, blank (no running heads) pages. Before you follow blindly behind major publishers, consider that they market to readers who often encounter the book *on a table in a bookstore.* The cover attracts a reader who reads the back, opens the book … and the first thing they see is positive reviews.

But if you're self-publishing and your book won't be displayed on a table in bookstores, consider skipping the opening praise. If you are able to collect endorsements from famous people, consider including these on your back cover and/or in the marketing blurb displayed in your book's online bookstore description.

The opening page is sometimes used for a promotional "blurb" or an excerpt—in paperbacks, a substitute for what would otherwise be printed on a jacket flap.

Ad Card

The optional Ad Card offers a list of other books written by the author.

When the Ad Card isn't part of the title spread,* it usually precedes it.

Some indie authors write to establish authority, leadership, and credibility in a given area. If you've previously written several books on a subject, an Ad Card can inspire confidence in readers.

Though the Ad Card is traditionally part of the Front Matter, readers will likely be more interested in your other work *after* you successfully engage them with the book they're reading. If you're not a famous writer and you want to include an Ad Card, consider moving it to the Back Matter.

If you're self-publishing, it's easy enough to upload revisions to accommodate literary fame when it inevitably occurs.

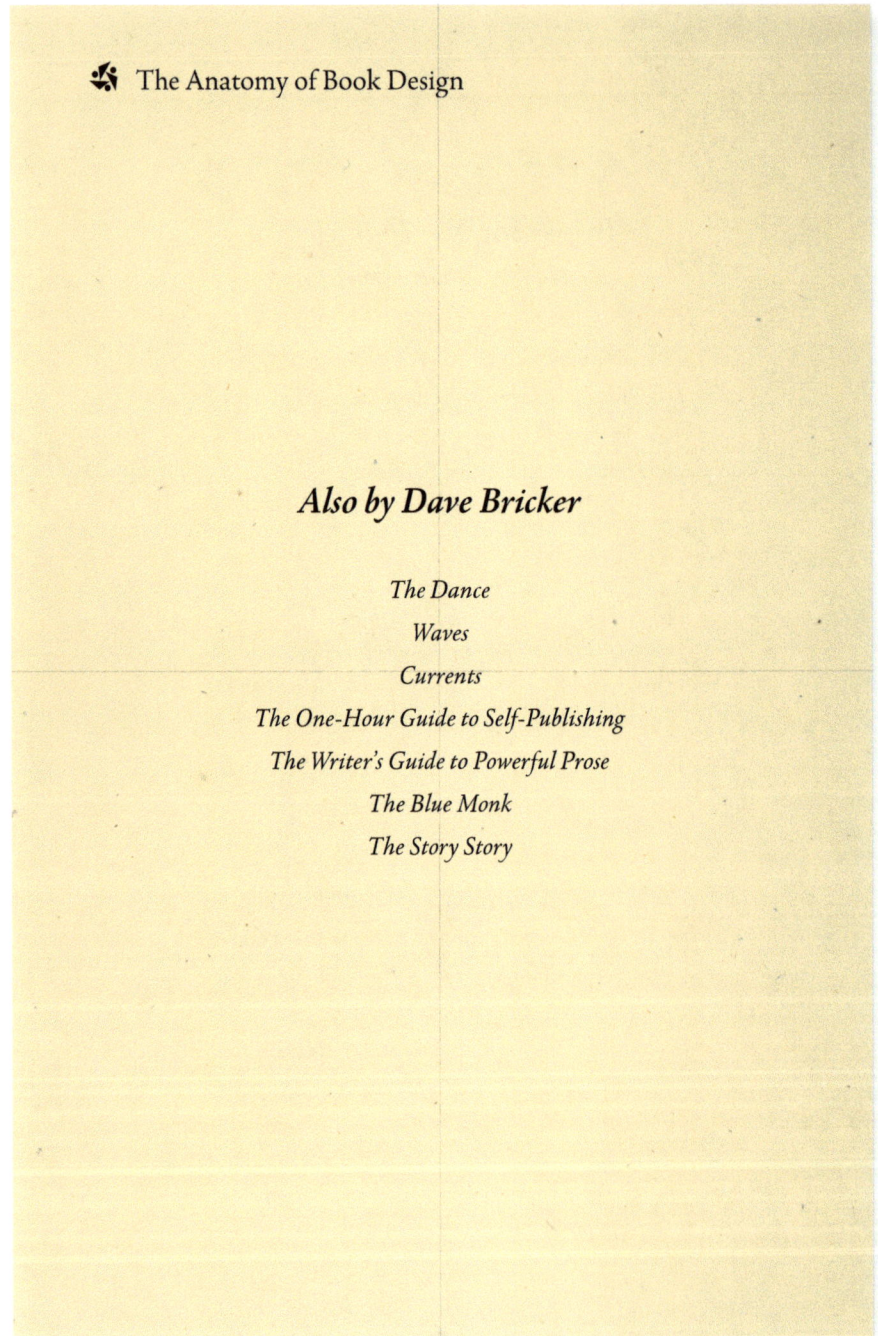

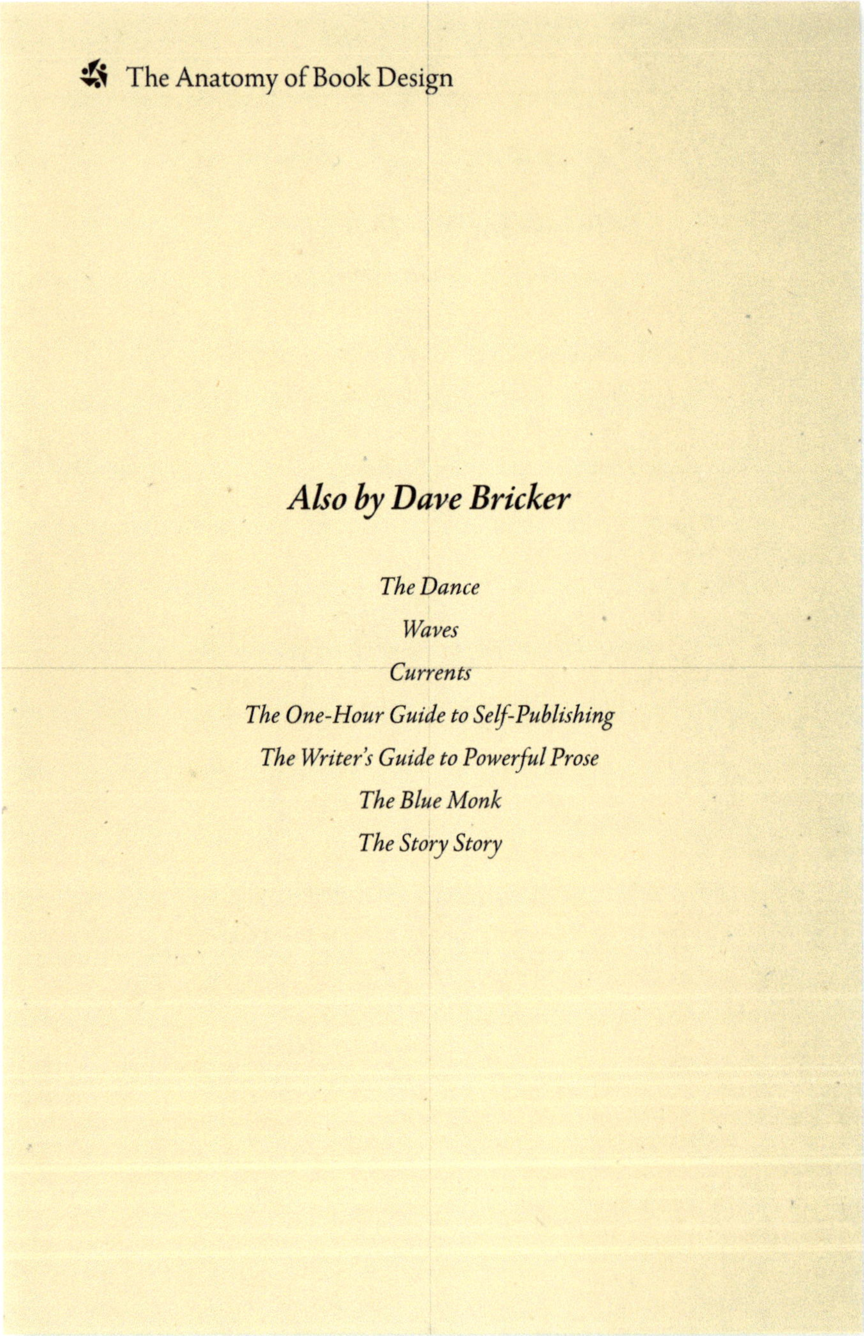

The Anatomy of Book Design
Also by Dave Bricker
The Dance
Waves
Currents
The One-Hour Guide to Self-Publishing
The Writer's Guide to Powerful Prose
The Blue Monk
The Story Story

*Two "facing" pages are called a "spread." The page on the left is a "verso" page, and the page on the right is a "recto" page.

Half-Title

Only the book's title and subtitle appear on a Half-Title page. This useless holdover from the days before books were bound with hard covers acts as an "opening" Title Page that precedes the "real" Title Page.

This may be a nod to tradition, but it serves little purpose to have two title pages. Presumably, the reader knows the title *before* they open the book. Reassuring them that the contents of the book is indeed what they expected seems a waste of paper. If you must include a Half-Title page, make it a right-hand (recto) page.

Frontispiece

The optional Frontispiece displays artwork related to the book's subject or a portrait of the author on the left ("verso") page facing the Title Page. A Frontspiece is rarely included in contemporary book design, but because it's a named component of traditional book anatomy, it's included in this reference.

If you elect not to include a Frontispiece, leave this page blank or use it for an Ad Card (see page 4).

William Caxton showing specimens of his printing to King Edward IV and his Queen. Published in *The Graphic* in 1877

The Publisher's Guide to

BOOK ANATOMY

BY DAVE BRICKER

ESSENTIAL ABSURDITIES PRESS

Title Page

The Title Page includes the author's name, the title, and the subtitle. The publisher's mark may appear at the bottom. Occasionally, an illustration is added. Traditionally, this is a right (recto) page with the Copyright Page on the back.

This is the proper place to sign your book—i.e. to place your signature under your printed name (usually with a slash through the print). Any inscription should be placed on an earlier recto page, such as the Half-Title page or a Blank page.

Publisher / Copyright

Publisher information appears on the back side of the title page, including the copyright notice, the ISBN (International Standard Book Number) and printing numbers, the publisher's address, the year(s) the book was published, and Library of Congress Catalogue information. Some authors credit their book's cover and interior designers here. The publisher's mark is often displayed.

It is not necessary to repeat the title and author on this page unless the author is the copyright holder. Fancy design is not required, either. This is *legal* language. Text can be set as small as needed as long as it's legible.

This book may not be reproduced, transmitted, or stored in whole or in part by any means, including graphic, electronic, or mechanical without the express written consent of the publisher except in the case of brief quotations embodied in critical articles and reviews.

Cover and book design by Dave Bricker.
ISBN: 978-0-9862960-1-7

© 2018
ESSENTIAL ABSURDITIES PRESS
Miami, FL

http://www.theworldsgreatestbook.com

printed in USA

To all those authors, publishers, and
designers who labor to make excellent books.

Dedication

The optional Dedication page is where the author dedicates the book to someone or something. You might dedicate your book to people in certain circumstances or to certain principles.

Use this section for *meaningful* messages; skip the niceties. Your readers will not be offended if you skip dedicating the book "to my loyal readers" in favor of getting on with it. The example on this page may make you feel good, but it adds another page that must be turned before you can start reading *the book*.

The Dedication traditionally follows the Copyright page.

Blank Pages

Don't be afraid to leave pages blank, even if you see big publishers starting chapters on left-hand (verso) pages. Most major book elements (with exceptions like the Copyright Page) traditionally start on right-hand (recto) pages. When printing tens of thousands of books at a time, publishers often break with tradition and omit blank pages to save money on paper and shipping.

If you are producing books with Print-On-Demand (POD) technology and the efficiencies of mass production are not your concern, consider that readers (even left-handed ones) "thumb" through a book from front to back with their right hand. Chapter starts and other elements that begin on right-hand pages are more visible and therefore easier to find.

Some publishers in certain circumstances feel the need to write "This page intenionally left blank" on "blank" pages. Not only is it safe to assume that your readers will not think blank pages are unintended, if you write *anything* on a page, it will no longer be blank despite any assertions you make to the contrary.

Table of Contents

Table of Contents

Known colloquially as the "TOC," the Table of Contents lists the sections, chapters, and other elements of the book along with the page where each begins. Not every book requires one. Readers of nonfiction reference books will find the table of contents more useful than readers of novels.

Consider whether the list of chapter titles inspires interest in the book. One of my clients recently published *7 Keys to Successful Relationships.* Her TOC offers readers a quick and useful guide to what they can expect to read inside the book. I included a TOC in my sailing memoir, *The Blue Monk,* because chapters like "Souls and Stories," and "Dog Patch" suggest the book will be a colorful reading experience.

Table of Contents

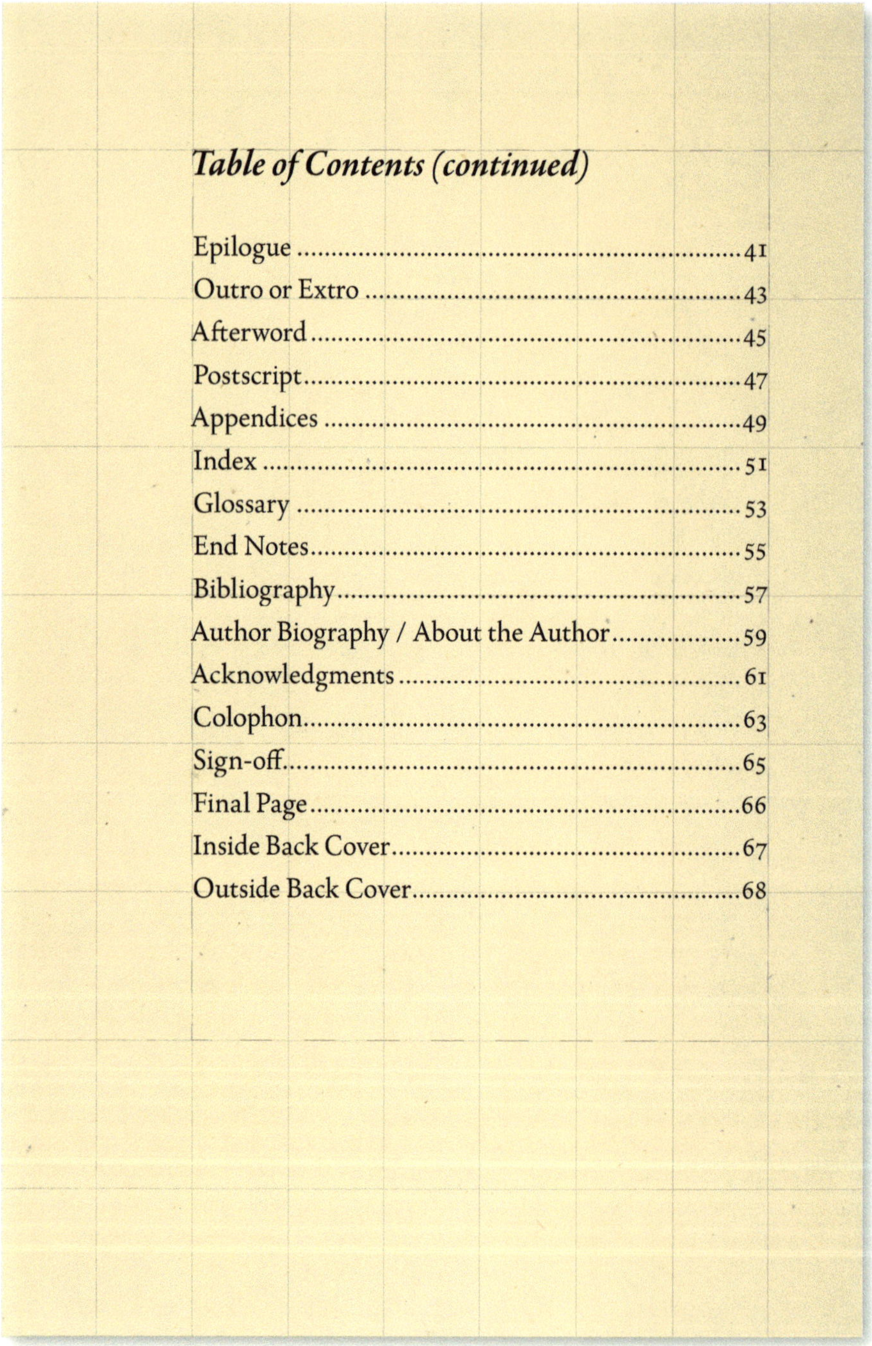

Table of Contents (continued)

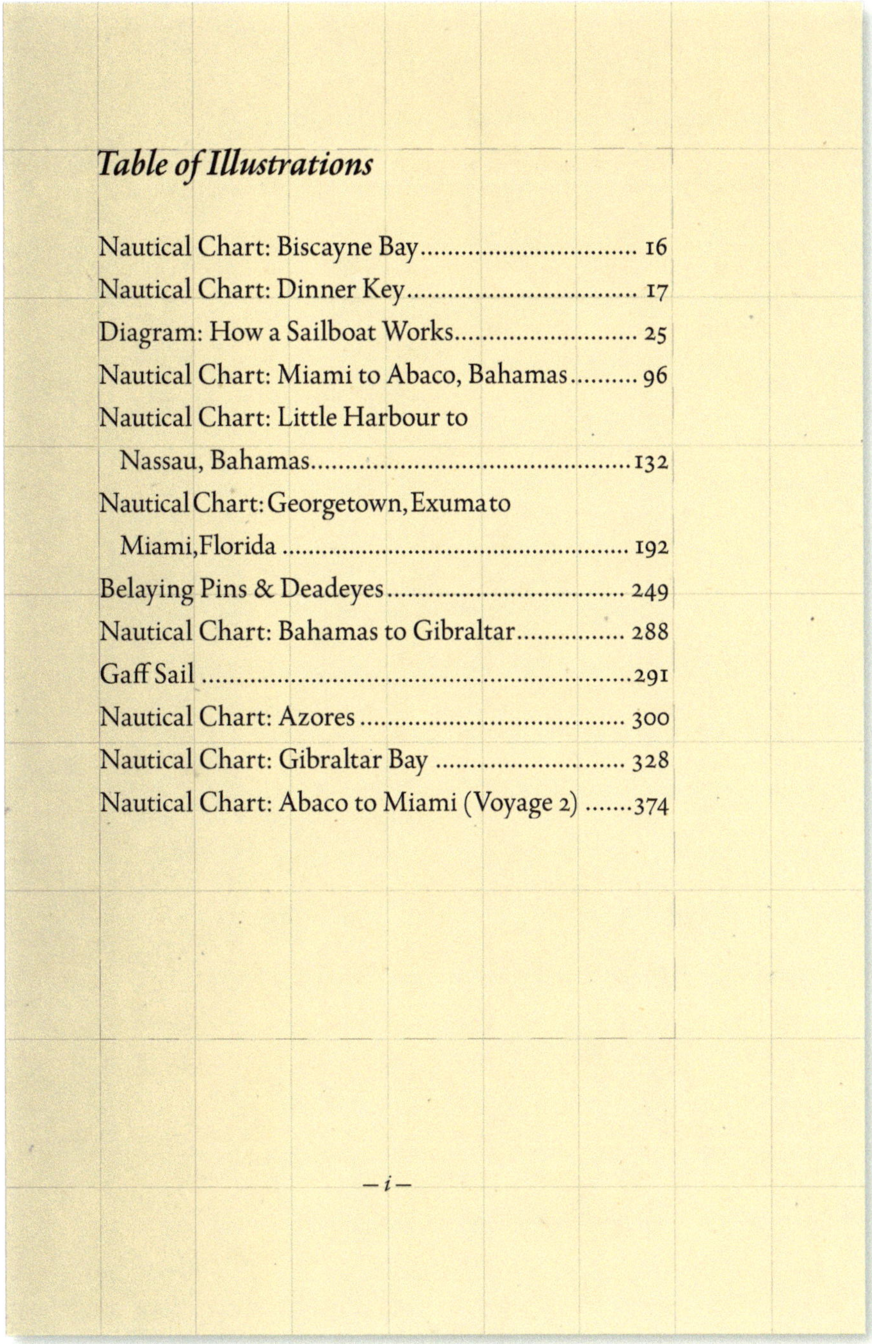

Table of Illustrations

Charts, Diagrams, Photos, and Illustrations are listed in the Table of Illustrations: If your book contains illustrations and you want readers to be able to find them quickly, include a separate table. If you offer charts or diagrams that provide useful statistics, include a Table of Illustrations so readers can quickly refer to them without having to recall what chapter they're associated with.

If your book contains illustrations that complement the narrative but don't offer much value on their own, this table is probably unnecessary.

Table of Illustrations

— *i* —

Table of Illustrations from my sailing memoir, *The Blue Monk,* 2014.

Foreword by Joseph Conrad

Dear Captain Sutherland,

When you first told me of your intention to publish a little book about the cruise of the *Ready* in October–November 1916, and asked me if I had any objection, I told you that it was not in my power to raise an effective objection, but that in any case the recollection of your kindness during those days when we were shipmates in the North Sea would have prevented me from putting as much as a formal protest in your way. Having taken that attitude, and the book being now ready for publication, I am glad of this opportunity of testifying to my regard for you, for Lieutenant Osborne, R.N.R., and for the naval and civilian crews of H.M. Brigantine *Ready* not forgetting Mr Moodie, the sailing master, whose sterling worth we all appreciated so much both as a seaman and as a shipmate.

I have no doubt that your memories are accurate, but as these are exclusively concerned with my person I am at liberty, without giving offence, to confess that I don't think they were worth preserving in print. But that is your affair. What this experience meant to me in its outward sensations and deeper feelings must remain my private possession.

— *v* —

Excerpt from Sutherland, John G. *At Sea with Joseph Conrad: With a Foreword by Joseph Conrad.* Grant Richards, Ltd. 1922. In this example, Conrad penned a Foreword for Sutherland's book about their time spent sailing together.

Foreword

Often misspelled 'forward,' this section preceding the main text is written by someone *other* than the author. If you're publishing an academic or business book, an introduction by a relevant thought leader or famous entrepreneur can encourage readers to take you seriously. If you write horror novels and can get Stephen King to write a few paragraphs explaining why fans of that genre should read your book, a Foreword can become a useful marketing tool. Get a famous scientist to write a Foreword for your science book. Get a former president to write a Foreword for your political analysis. If the writer of your Foreword has no clout with your intended audience, consider leaving it out.

Preface

A Preface explains how your book came to be. It is similar to a Foreword, but is written by you, the author.

If one day you found yourself clinging to a high mountainside, cowering in a foxhole, in love with someone from a "forbidden" culture, or playing guitar for change on the streets of Gibraltar, you may have experienced one of those moments when you knew you had a story to tell. It's preferable to tell that story within your narrative, but if your book is about your present-day medical practice, your experiences as a medic in the Vietnam War might best be included as a preface. Readers will understand a bit more about the forces that shaped you personally and professionally, but they'll be less confused when you jump from a tent in the Mekong Delta in 1968 to an operating room in Chicago in 2015.

Think of a Preface as *personal* backstory and a Prologue (see page 33) as *historical* backstory.

Preface

At eighteen, I found myself living in the storybook world of Miami's Dinner Key Anchorage, a floating Tortilla Flat offering colorful characters, fascinating sailing craft, and the world's largest back yard. Inspired, and knowing I would one day write a book about my own adventures, I took photographs and kept a journal.

Aboard my boat *The Blue Monk,* my wanderings soon took me past my home on Biscayne Bay to the magic islands of the Bahamas just beyond the mighty Gulf Stream. Alone in the islands, I learned to spear fish, set my sails, and navigate through reefs and shoals.

In 1991, I joined a friend for a 38-day Atlantic crossing where we encountered peaceful calms, a terrifying storm or two, and the volcanic islands of the Azores.

It wasn't until twenty years later that I published my memoir, *The Blue Monk,* but by that time, I had already established my publishing consultancy and book design practice.

The *Publisher's Guide to Book Anatomy* was inspired by my journeys in search of stories and by my studies of the wordcraft required to tell those stories well. It is my hope that this book empowers you to communicate your own

— *vii* —

First page of an example Preface composed for this book.

Introduction

You have something to say—a story to tell, a message for the world, a new idea, or a memory to share. You sit down and begin to type. As ideas flow, you research all those things you wish you'd paid attention to in high school: how to use a semicolon, how many spaces to type after a period (one), how to properly use an em-dash or ellipsis, and all the arcana associated with becoming a writer.

You find reference books for grammar and style, consult your thesaurus and dictionary, perhaps experiment with writing software, and slowly convert your ideas into squiggly marks on a screen.

As your manuscript turns into a book, you look for guidance. What is a Preface? How is it different than a Foreword? What material goes in an Appendix or an Epilogue?

This book offers a simple book anatomy reference for writers, publishers, book designers, and editors. The material on the 'inner' pages offers an example of each type of section. The material in the outer margins discusses what the section should and should not contain.

You own a dictionary, a thesaurus, and a style manual. Add *The Indie Publisher's Guide to Book Anatomy* to your publishing reference library to help ensure publishing professionalism.

— *ix* —

First page of an example Introduction composed for this book.

Introduction

Prefaces, Forewords, and Prologues are all forms of Introductions, but a section given the formal name of "Introduction" can be likened to the opening slide of a presentation. Explain what will be covered, who the intended reader is, and what they can expect to get out of your book.

Authors ask readers to invest money and time in what they have to say. Your Introduction qualifies your book for your reader and explains why it's a good investment.

What can your reader expect to do with the knowledge you'll teach them? Will they use your lessons to fulfill creative goals, or will they enhance their career options? What's different about your book and your approach? Let target readers know you understand their culture and the challenges they face. In storytelling terms, assure them that your information will produce the desired transformation.

Editors' Note

THE SERIES OF CRITICAL bibliographies of French literature undertaken by the Syracuse University Press is widely recognized as the standard reference work of its type in the field. The guiding principle of the work is that of critical selectivity: the series provides for the specialist and advanced student of French literature bibliographical information about those books and articles of which he or he should be aware in the pursuit of further study. Insofar as possible, the bibliographies attempt to present an objective survey of various specialized fields by scholars known in the United States and Europe for their particular interest or competence with regard to a given subject or author. Moreover, every collaborator has worked in close consultation with the volume editor. Nevertheless, in a work of this scope and complexity, errors or omissions are bound to occur. The editors urge all users of this work to call them to their attention, as it is our hope that the material presented in this volume may be brought up to date periodically.

The period since 1960 has been marked by a great flourishing of studies of seventeenth-century French literature both in Europe and in the United States. The purpose of the present work is to survey that body of scholarship in

— *xi* —

Excerpt from Editors' (plural) Note: Cabeen, David Clark, and Richard A. Brooks. *A Critical Bibliography of French Literature.* Syracuse University Press, 1968. Here, the editors comment on a newly published version of an estabished reference book for French literary scholars.

Editor's Note

An Editor's Note or Publisher's Note is used to provide information abut the text beyond what the author(s) included.

If the text is a new edition or a fresh translation of an old work, the editor or publisher may wish to discuss the research and scholarship behind it.

An Editor's Note might comment on why the world needs yet another edition of *Moby-Dick*. Reasons could include new research that revealed insights about the author and the book, remarks about the book's design, or suggestions that current events give the book a new relevance.

An editor or publisher might also comment on a compilation or anthology.

Editor's Notes are routinely included in magazines and periodicals where the editor acts as a "host" or "emcee."

"Outside of a dog, a book is a man's best friend. Inside of a dog it's too dark to read."

– Groucho Marx

Epigraph

An optional Epigraph is a short quotation or saying at the beginning of a book or chapter. Like the dedication, it usually falls on a right-hand (recto) page just before the actual storytelling begins. When used to start a chapter, it's usually set in italics at the start of the chapter. The chapter content follows after a double line break or chapter ornament.

An epigraph can set the tone for a book by introducing a clever thought or a philosophical undertone. If you quote Lao Tzu or Oscar Wilde or Mark Twain (or Groucho Marx), readers will make inferences about your writing style and influences.

Section II
Book Matter

Book Matter is the "heart" of a book—the actual story or informational text that lies between the Front Matter and the Back Matter. The Front Matter introduces the book, and the Back Matter closes the book. The Book Matter *is* the book.

Parts, Sections, and Chapters

Depending on the complexity of the subject matter, a book may be subdivided into Parts, Sections, and Chapters.

The Bible (usually bound as a single volume) is divided into two "Testaments" (analogous to "Parts"). Each contains dozens of Books, and each Book contains multiple Chapters. These are further divided into "Verses" that each contain roughly one independent clause.

Parts: A "Part" may be an entirely separate volume (*Harry Potter and the Sorcerer's Stone* is Part I of J.K. Rowling's multipart story) or it might be a major content division within a book.

Sections are used to divide books that contain chapters that fall into logical groupings. In this book, the various elements of book anatomy are grouped into three sections: Front Matter, Body Matter, and Back Matter. This division offers a logical classification system that allows readers to find content quickly or understand your narrative more readily.

Book matter pages are numbered with Arabic numerals that start with "1" on the first page of the first chapter.

The Publisher's Guide to
BOOK ANATOMY

Second Half-Title

Include an optional Half-Title page between the front matter and the Book Matter. This tells readers where the "official" beginning of the book is after you've ignored this book's advice and packed thirty pages of Front Matter in before the main narrative begins.

Running Heads display the chapter or section name, except on pages where the chapter is already named, in which case they refer to the author. Here, the author's name is used instead of repeating "Prologue" which is already on the page. Running heads on left-hand (verso) pages display the book's title. Sometimes (as in this book's main narrative), page numbers are included in the running heads.

Dave Bricker ❦

Prologue

Despite the explosion in publishing, book design is a lost art. For centuries, printing was a craft practiced by trained artisans who served long apprenticeships before becoming master printers.

The "desktop publishing" revolution changed that overnight. Amateurs began to create book layouts without any knowledge of typefaces and traditional design strategies.

"Big box" bookstores and the Internet brought on a wave of design compromises – sacrifices to the gods of mass production. Type grew smaller and margins grew narrower to save ink, paper, and shipping costs on boxcar-sized printing runs.

A new generation of digital designers swarmed in to replace those who had worked with the ancient art of hot metal type – and this generation was left to rediscover the lost wisdom on its own.

Though this book hardly touches on aesthetic design, it offers a useful and necessary guide to book anatomy for amateur and professional publishers alike. Even if you formally studied publication design, chances are good that the details of printed book design were overlooked in your training. If you're a writer or editor, time spent exploring

First page of an example Prologue composed for this book.

Prologue

An optional Prologue is used primarily in fiction. Place it before the beginning of a story to introduce characters or provide important background information. If your story takes place during the Crimean War or in 18th-century Ireland, a prologue will help your reader understand your story in its intended historical context. Keep it brief. And because many readers will skip it, reveal historical information within the narrative itself when you can.

The imagined Prologue on this example page offers a historical justification for this book.

The Prologue is traditionally considered Front Matter, but it's referenced here in the Book Matter section because readers may have difficulty understanding your story if they skip it. Consider including it *inside* your book *after* the second Half-Title Page to help ensure it gets read.

Think of a Preface as *personal* backstory and a Prologue as *historical* backstory

An Initial Capital or "Drop-Cap" at a chapter start is often followed by a word or phrase set in all-capitals

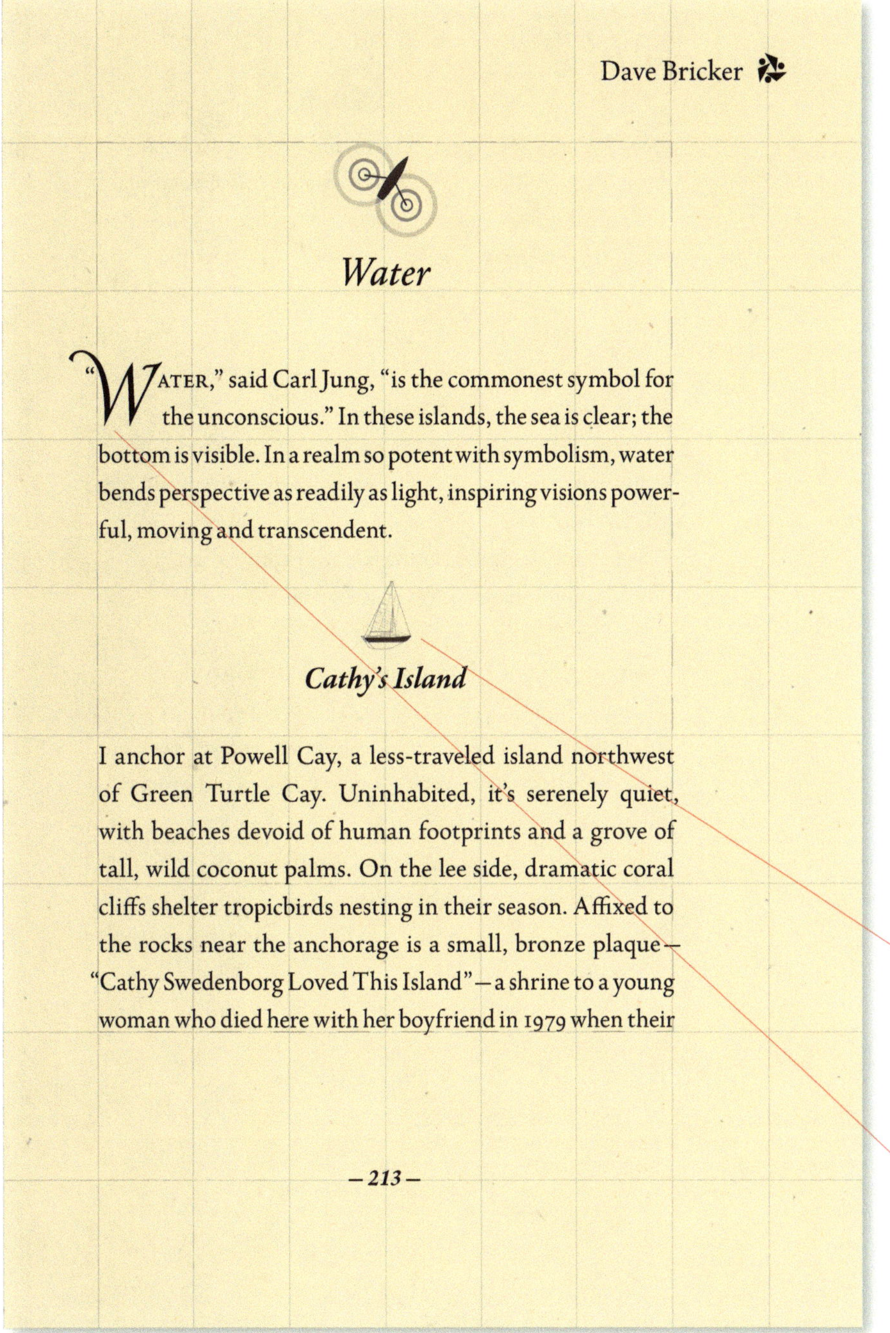

Dave Bricker

Water

"WATER," said Carl Jung, "is the commonest symbol for the unconscious." In these islands, the sea is clear; the bottom is visible. In a realm so potent with symbolism, water bends perspective as readily as light, inspiring visions powerful, moving and transcendent.

Cathy's Island

I anchor at Powell Cay, a less-traveled island northwest of Green Turtle Cay. Uninhabited, it's serenely quiet, with beaches devoid of human footprints and a grove of tall, wild coconut palms. On the lee side, dramatic coral cliffs shelter tropicbirds nesting in their season. Affixed to the rocks near the anchorage is a small, bronze plaque—"Cathy Swedenborg Loved This Island"—a shrine to a young woman who died here with her boyfriend in 1979 when their

– *213* –

Sample chapter pages taken from my sailing memoir, *The Blue Monk,* 2014. This chapter offers several vignettes on the theme of "Water," each of which is preceded by a chapter ornament and a subtitle.

Chapters

Chapters are to a book as a paragraph is to an essay. Each Chapter focuses on a particular piece of information, a step in a process, a particular concept that's part of a book's larger message, or a finite chunk of a story that moves the narrative forward.

In this book, each individual component of Book Anatomy is given its own (usually one-page) Chapter.

Book designers typically start chapters with a headline. Text sometimes begins farther down than on a standard page of text and then continues at the top of subsequent pages. Some publishers use Chapter Ornaments to help delineate where Chapters begin. Section Ornaments and/or subheadlines delineate Section starts. Text starting a Chapter may contain an Initial Capital (Drop-Cap) and or a capitalized word or phrase.

The Blue Monk

boat burned. Her epitaph is unconcerned with what was lost. Instead, it connects her forever to this special place she found and appreciated, and to her enduring suggestion that I might love it, too.

Late at night, I awaken and step into the cockpit. Unadulterated by urban incandescence, untinted by the azure hue of day, the nocturnal world projects its magic for those fortunate to bear witness.

The moon is high and bright; the white sand bottom illuminated like a stadium; the lunar light brilliant enough to read by.

I step astern, grabbing the backstay for support.

A diamond shape moves in the water below me.

And another.

Giant Atlantic stingrays glide over the bottom: dozens of them. Their dark forms undulate, slow and graceful against brilliant, subaquatic sand; an Escher woodcut brought to life; a moving tapestry of figure and ground; a dream landscape.

Such sights may be common. Stingrays may congregate here regularly on moonlit nights – or perhaps – only once – tonight. It doesn't matter; I am blessed to witness a secret world of shadows and light.

– *214* –

A Note About Copyfitting

The typesetter's goal is to ensure that facing pages have the same number of lines whenever possible, except at the end of a chapter (as in this example spread). There is room on this left-hand (verso) page for one more line of type, but this would leave the last line of the paragraph orphaned on the facing

Dave Bricker

Cathy Swedenborg loved this island.
I understand.

– 215 –

(recto) page. By adding or removing a line from facing pages, the incidence of orphans (last line of a paragraph at the top of a page) and widows (first line of a paragraph at the bottom of a page) is reduced. When necessary, character spacing and even character width can be adjusted to ensure that type is balanced and typeset according to best practices. Additional techniques include tightening a paragraph to reduce its length by a line, or bumping the last two words to a new line to lengthen it.

Chapters

The final page of a Chapter should contain at least two lines.

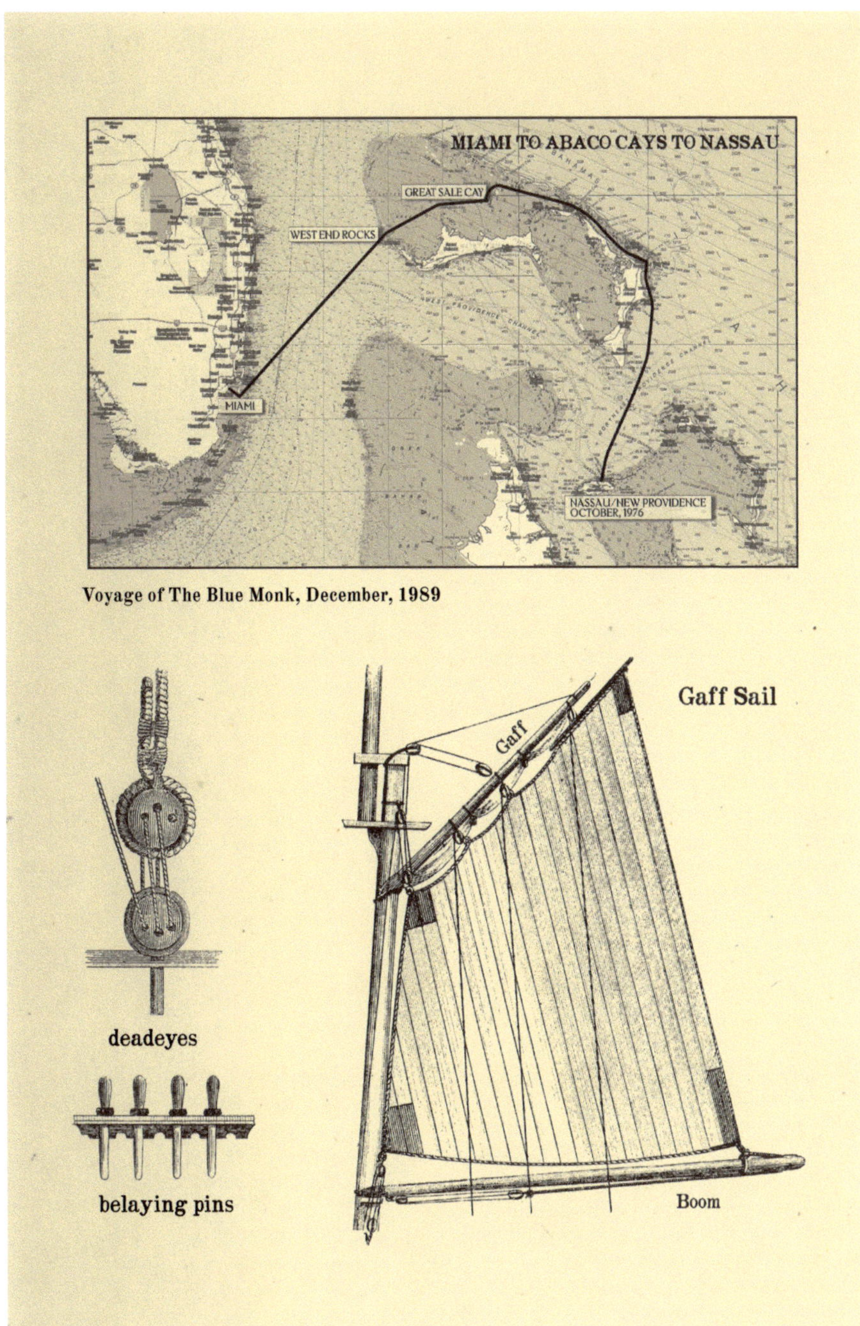

Sample Art Program for an imagined book about a sailing voyage.

Art Program

An Art Program includes photographs and galleries, illustrations, tables, graphs, et cetera. The Art Program often appears in separate "signatures" such as when a book is divided by one or more "photo sections."

Art Program pages generally lack page numbers and running heads. Continue page numbering when the narrative resumes without counting the Art Program pages. Think of these sections as if they were *inserted* into the completed book.

Section III

Back Matter

Any content that lies between "The End" and the Back Cover is considered "Back Matter."

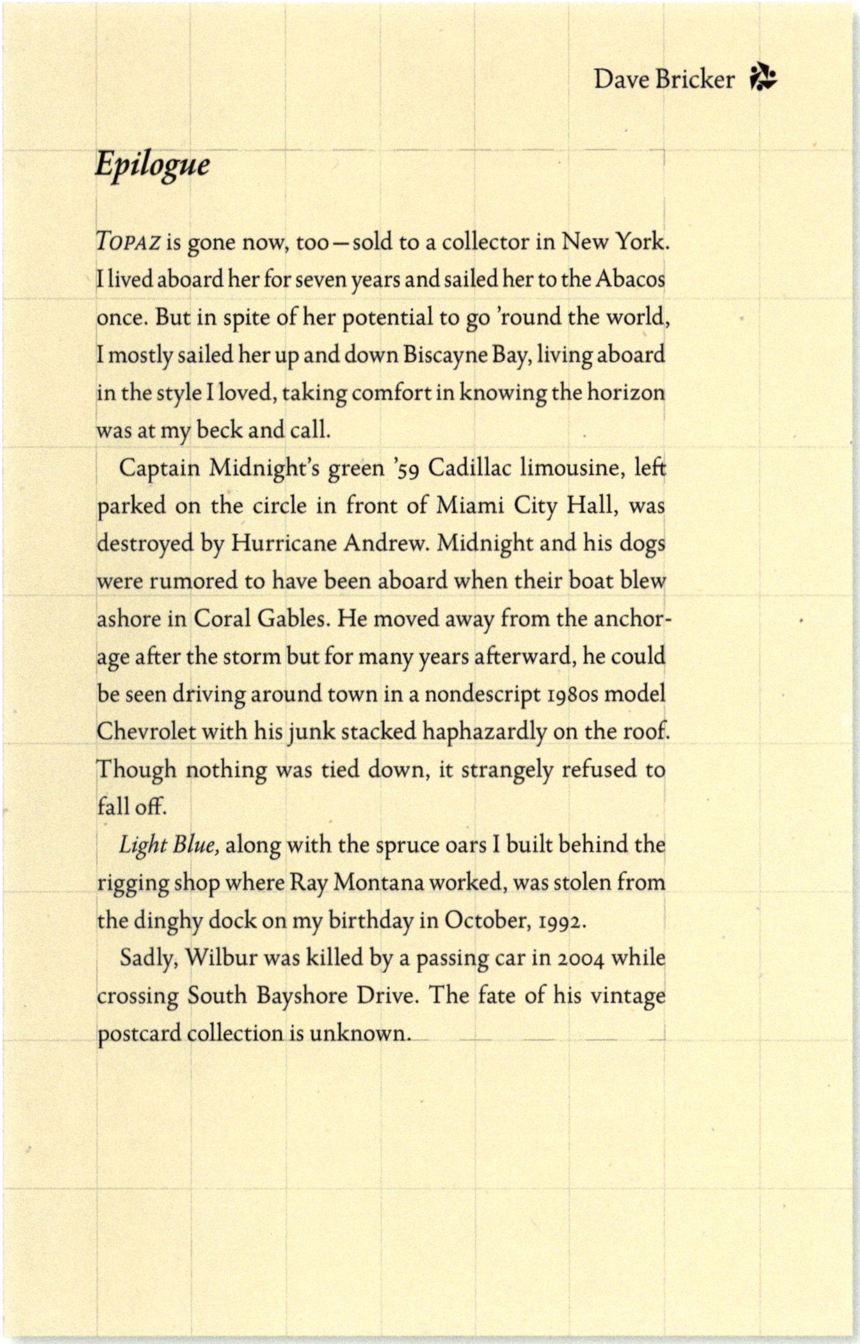

Dave Bricker

Epilogue

TOPAZ is gone now, too—sold to a collector in New York. I lived aboard her for seven years and sailed her to the Abacos once. But in spite of her potential to go 'round the world, I mostly sailed her up and down Biscayne Bay, living aboard in the style I loved, taking comfort in knowing the horizon was at my beck and call.

Captain Midnight's green '59 Cadillac limousine, left parked on the circle in front of Miami City Hall, was destroyed by Hurricane Andrew. Midnight and his dogs were rumored to have been aboard when their boat blew ashore in Coral Gables. He moved away from the anchorage after the storm but for many years afterward, he could be seen driving around town in a nondescript 1980s model Chevrolet with his junk stacked haphazardly on the roof. Though nothing was tied down, it strangely refused to fall off.

Light Blue, along with the spruce oars I built behind the rigging shop where Ray Montana worked, was stolen from the dinghy dock on my birthday in October, 1992.

Sadly, Wilbur was killed by a passing car in 2004 while crossing South Bayshore Drive. The fate of his vintage postcard collection is unknown.

First page of the Epilogue from my book, *The Blue Monk,* 2104.

Epilogue

An Epilogue is analogous to a Prologue. It's used in storytelling to provide a conclusion when parts of a story are left hanging. Just as there are Prefaces and Prologues, there are Postfaces and Epilogues, though these are often both labeled "Epilogue" (and Postfaces are rare). If you want to provide *historical* developments that come after your story in an Epilogue, and *personal* developments that come after the story in a Postface, you can attempt to impress readers with your erudition (or not). Avoid spoilers in case someone reads your Epilogue before reading the story.

Epilogues are ideal for "Where are they now?" content. If you want to reveal what happened to your characters *after* the end of the story, an Epilogue offers an ideal place to do so.

The Anatomy of Book Design

Dave Bricker

Outro

This *Indie Publisher's Guide to Book Anatomy* explores the names, locations, and purposes of the various components that make up a book. Though it's a valuable technical reference, consider its potential to inspire you on your writer's journey. Writing is the translation of intangible abstractions—thoughts, ideas, experiences, and memories—into physical, sharable form—ink and paper. An understanding of Book Anatomy empowers you to separate story from backstory. Considering your text in light of what material *is* the message and what material is *about* the message brings clarity and focus to your work.

The independent publisher is often an independent *author* who endeavors to transform a manuscript into a completed book. As publishers, today's writers assume roles traditionally practiced by printers, typographers, graphic designers, and merchants. The ability to distinguish between and properly include (or omit) a Preface, a Foreword, a Prologue, and an Introduction is as much a part of publishing professionalism as it is a part of writing professionalism.

As you shepherd your manuscript through the writing and editing process, consider how an understanding of Book Anatomy will reflect on your reader's ultimate perception

First page of an example Outro composed for this book.

Outro or Extro

An Outro is the opposite of an Introduction. If you wish to recap what your book covered—as you might when giving a lecture or presentation—an Outro can reinforce key concepts and remind your reader that you covered all the concepts you stated you'd cover at the beginning of the book.

What is it you want your reader to *do* with your material once they've completed reading? Readers are more likely to apply material they not only understand, but value. An Outro offers the writer an opportunity to reinforce the *transformation*—the "happily ever after" that results from the reader engaging with the information in your book.

The Anatomy of Book Design

Dave Bricker

AFTERWORD

Even as a young man, before his marriage into the gentry and ascension to the planter class, Simms shared the tidewater Southerner's "characteristic bias in favor of seaboard culture," viewing with "fundamental distrust" the "craving for land [and] wealth" that fostered the migration westward over the Appalachians.[1] In 1831, for instance, he voiced suspicion that "the possession of so much territory" was "greatly inimical to the well being of this country:" The constant "pull [ing] up [of] stakes and boom[ing] off for the new Canaan," Simms contended, not only "prevents the formation of society" but also "destroys that which is already well established" (L, I, 37). Despite his personal preference to remain in the South Carolina low country (he rejected the offer by his father to make him wealthy and politically prominent in Mississippi), the realistic-minded Simms recognized the inevitability of westward expansion in the development of the nation. Furthermore, in demonstration of a literary progressiveness in contrast with his conservatism in politics and economics, he identified the frontier as a dynamic, increasingly important topic with which to capture the imagination of the largely urban-based reading public. His timing in 1834 was perfect; *Guy Rivers* came off the press in New York just when America-in-literature was becoming a national demand; and the gold rush in the outlaw-dominated Georgia backwoods provided strikingly different subject matter.

Afterword from Simms, William Gilmore. *Guy Rivers; a Tale of Georgia*. Harper, 1934. In this example, the book was originally published in 1834. This Afterword, written when the book was reissued a hundred years later, offers commentary on the political and literary landscape at the time of the volume's first publication.

Afterword

An Afterword is similar to a Foreword. It consists of remarks about the book *written by someone other than the author.* Putting this content in the Back Matter means your reader gets to your content faster, but it also means they might miss an important discussion or endorsement that would otherwise compel them to purchase the book, give you more credence as an author, or understand it more deeply.

Another purpose of an Afterword is to provide a response to critical remarks made about a previous edition.

Don't misspell "Afterword" as "Afterward."

The Anatomy of Book Design

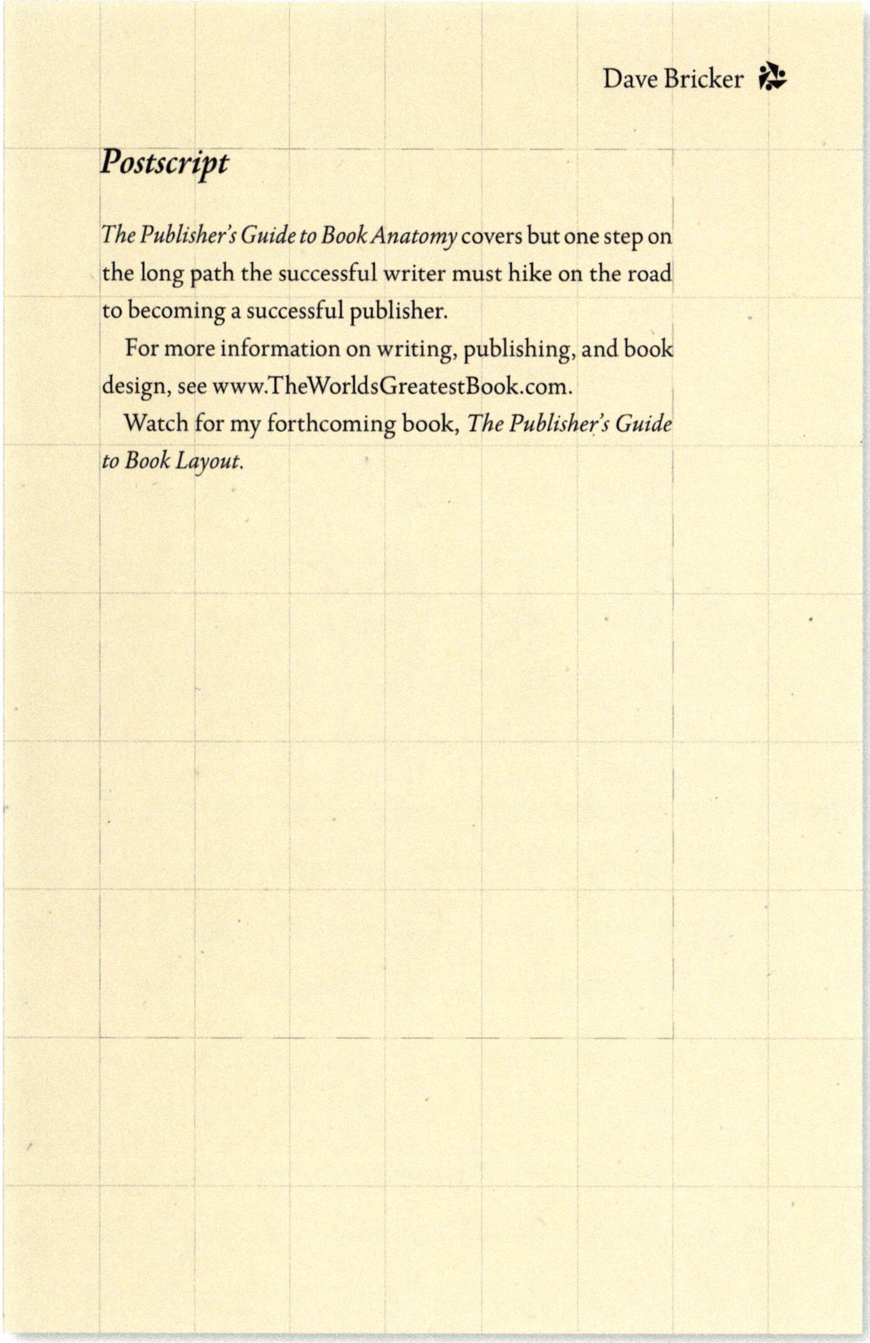

Postscript

Rarely used, a postscript provides information about the preceding text, and possibly offers brief information about a sequel or related material.

Dave Bricker

Postscript

The Publisher's Guide to Book Anatomy covers but one step on the long path the successful writer must hike on the road to becoming a successful publisher.

For more information on writing, publishing, and book design, see www.TheWorldsGreatestBook.com.

Watch for my forthcoming book, *The Publisher's Guide to Book Layout.*

Example Postscript composed for this book.

The Anatomy of Book Design

Dave Bricker

Appendix 1: Choosing a Book Font

Selecting a book font seems simple enough, but fine points of typography are not obvious to many authors. This appendix offers insights into fonts suitable for book typography. Though it won't turn you into a professional typesetter, it will inform indie publishers about the kind of guidance they should expect to receive from one. And if economic constraints force you to typeset your own book, the information offered here will help you make informed choices.

Book typography is an unusual art. Its success is best measured by the *invisibility* of the final result. The reader should not notice the type, and the type should not obscure or dilute the author's intentions. Yet, the reader should be *affected* by the type. Reading is an aesthetic experience, and book font selection lies at its foundation.

Choosing a Book Font: Why Bother?

Choose a book font to set the tone for your book. In our data-driven age, it's too easy to focus on simply getting information onto the page. Type has a functional role to play, and it doesn't have to do much more than be legible to accomplish that goal. But the highest compliment I'm paid as a designer is when someone opens one of my books and

First page of an example Appendix composed for this book. (Book layout will be covered in a forthcoming book.)

Appendices

Nonfiction books may have one or more Appendices offering recommended books, websites, organizations, or other resources related to the book. An Appendix may also offer material that's too granular or tangential to the book's main topic. By moving this material to an Appendix, it becomes supplemental or optional reading that doesn't bog down the flow or simplicity of the main narrative.

Novels or books of stories rarely include appendices, though it's conceivable that one might offer recipes corresponding to dishes made by a character who cooks in the story, or plans for craft projects made by a carpenter character.

Appendix material isn't part of the story, but it offers a way to bring the story into a reader's life .

The Anatomy of Book Design

Dave Bricker

Index

First page of an example Index composed for this book.

Index

An Index is most commonly found in nonfiction books. Words and terms are listed alphabetically with corresponding page numbers. In a cookbook, for example, readers can quickly find pages/recipes that correspond to terms like "pastry flour" or "apple" or "peanut butter."

If there are multiple references throughout the book, the page numbers are separated by commas, or—if several pages together make reference, they are separated by an en-dash. To wit: 4, 7, 8–9, 14

The Anatomy of Book Design

Glossary

Usually found in nonfiction books, a glossary is essentially a dictionary containing terms and definitions of words found in the book. A nautical book, for example, might include terms like "port and starboard," "mast," and "bowsprit" in a glossary to make the book easier for non-sailors to understand. Looking up words in a glossary is faster and more convenient than finding them in a separate dictionary, and it's less confusing as only relevant definitions are included.

Dave Bricker

Glossary

Acknowledgments	A section paying homage to those who contibuted to the book or inspired the author to write it.
Ad Card	A section listing other books by the author.
Back Matter	Content that lies between the end of the main narrative and the back cover.
Book Matter	Content that lies between the front matter and the back matter; the main narrative.
Chapters	Chapters divide the main narrative into "lessons" or stopping points.
Copyright Page	Provides information about the publisher, copyrights, and other legal information describing the book as a piece of intellectual property and who owns it.
Dedication Page	An author's short homage to a source of inspiration or object of affection.
Epigraph	A quotation at the beginning of a book or chapter that sets the tone for the narrative.
Foreword	An introduction to the book written by someone other than the author.
Front Matter	Content that lies between the front cover and the main narrative.
Frontispiece	An illustration or portrait of the author preceding the title page.

First page of an example Glossary composed for this book.

The Anatomy of Book Design

Dave Bricker

End Notes

Army

1. Jamea LeMoyne, "Central America's Arms Build up :" The Risks of Guns
2. "Without Butter," The New York Times, April 19, 1987.
3. "High Honduran Officers Ousted," The New York Times, September 30, 1986.

FUSEP and Physical Integrity

4. "Rebel band seeks Honduras toehold," *The Miami Herald,* November 7, 1986.
5. *FBIS,* quoting *Tiempo* March 3, 1986, p. 20.
6. *Tiempo,* July 9, 1986.
7. *El Heraldo,* July 9, 1986.
8. *La Tribuna,* May 17, 1986 .
9. *El Heraldo,* July 19, 1986.
10. *Tiempo,* May 29, 1986.
11. *Tiempo,* July 19, 1986.
12. *La Tribuna,* August 7, 1986.
13. *Tiempo,* July 30, 1986.
14. *Tiempo,* March 18 and 19, 1986.
15. *Tiempo,* April 22, 1986.
16. *La Tribuna,* February 5, 1987.

Partial Endnotes from Manuel, Anne. "Endnotes." Human Rights in Honduras: Central America's 'Sideshow', *Americas Watch,* 1987, p. 144. Though this example is not particularly interesting to read, it allows the main text to remain uncluttered by footnotes. Readers wishing to research the book's sources can find the numbered references in the End Notes.

End Notes

End Notes are used at the end of a book to accomplish the same goals as footnotes. End Notes are less intrusive than footnotes, but are less likely to be read because readers have to jump to the back of the book to find them.

Footnotes are used at the bottom (foot) of a page to expand on topics raised on the same page. Each note is connected by a reference number to a corresponding number within the main text. Footnotes can include bibliographies, links, explanations of terms, and brief background information that doesn't belong in the main text. If you need more than a few on any page, consider using End Notes. Too many footnotes create clutter, typographical mayhem, and distractions from the text.

Various house styles (Chicago and MLA, for example) define proper formats for Footnotes and End Notes.

Footnotes have become a defining characteristic of some postmodern fiction (David Foster Wallace; Dave Eggers). Some contain mini-essays on material that would otherwise interrupt the flow of the book.

The Anatomy of Book Design

Dave Bricker

Bibliography

Orcutt, William Dana, and Edward Everett Bartlett. *The Manual of Linotype Typography: Prepared to Aid Users and Producers of Printing in Securing Greater Unity and Real Beauty in the Printed Page.* Mergenthaler Linotype Co., 1923.

Lee, Marshall. *Bookmaking: Editing, Design, Production.* W.W. Norton & Company, 2004.

Haslam, Andrew. *Bookdesign:* Abrams, 2006.

Hendel, Richard. *On Book Design.* Yale University Press, 2006.

Sutherland, John G. *At Sea with Joseph Conrad: With a Foreword by Joseph Conrad.* Grant Richards, Ltd. 1922.

Bibliography of references used while creating this book.

Bibliography

A Bibliography is a list of references used in writing the book. Sources can include books, articles, websites, audio recordings, films, and other media.

Many publishers prefer to list sources as Footnotes on the pages where they occur, but if pages refer to too many sources or sources are referred to over and over, Footnoted sources can become confusing or too numerous to fit comfortably on the page.

As with End Notes, a Bibliography can reduce page clutter at the expense of forcing the reader to flip to the back of the book to find a referenced source. Bibliographies are often included in the End Notes section, but if a book contains numerous sources and also includes numerous bits of supplemental information, consider putting notes and sources in separate sections to avoid numbering challenges.

Various house styles (Chicago and MLA, for example) define proper formats for Bibliographies.

The Anatomy of Book Design

Author Biography / About the Author

If you did your writing job well, readers will want to learn more about who entertained, enlightened, educated, or inspired them.

Keep your Author Biography brief and relevant. If you have a long personal story, write a separate memoir. If you wrote a book about business, talk about your entrepreneurial pursuits. Add a drop or two of personal interest material to help catalyze the "cult of personality" around your ideas and round out your reader's picture of you as an "interesting person."

Think about your goals as an author. If you wrote your book to establish credibility that wins you consulting or speaking work, let readers know what services you offer or audiences you speak to.

Avoid being overtly commercial. Readers who finish your book already trust your expertise and leadership. A sales pitch will not be required to induce them to initiate contact.

Dave Bricker

About the Author

Dave Bricker is a speaker, writer, editor, web designer, MFA graphic designer, and publishing consultant.

He taught graphic and web design and thesis writing at Miami International University of Art & Design for fourteen years and started his design studio, Spot Grafix, Inc., in 1995.

In 2014, he created the <PubML>® eBook platform, a web-based eBook format that delivers a more book-like reading experience than conventional eBooks. Included is a set of intuitive, visual tools that allows any author to produce elegant eBooks both for the web and for traditional eReaders.

Dave Bricker sailed thousands of solo miles in the late 1980s and then crossed the Atlantic Ocean in 1991. His sailing memoir, *The Blue Monk,* won an IPPY Award for excellence in Independent Publishing in 2015.

Visit www.TheWorldsGreatestBook.com, his award-winning website, for more information about writing, publishing, and book design. See DaveBricker.com for information about his speaking and consulting services.

Dave Bricker lives with his wife, daughter, and three rescue dogs in Miami, Florida. He plays guitar in a swing band and "helps remarkable people tell remarkable stories."

Sample Author Biography created for this book.

Acknowledgments

This book would not have been possible without inspiration from the many book and type designers who came before me. Claude Garamond, William Caslon, Eric Gill, Paul Renner, Milton Glaser, and Richard Hendel represent only a small selection of the many designers who inspired and empowered me to pursue the craft of bookmaking.

The craft of book design would be nothing without the craft of writing. I wish to convey my deepest gratitude to Stephen Bauer, who showed me the inestimable value of an insightful and encouraging, but honest editor.

No learning process is so powerful as *doing.* To the many authors who have trusted me to edit your manuscripts, set your type, create your book covers, and coach you through the publishing process, you have given me the gift of experience. I am honored to have been chosen to find wings for your words.

Thanks to Scott Miller and Dr. Margarita Gurri for test-reading this book's manuscript. Your comments, suggestions, and friendship were valuable contributions.

And of course, a list of acknowledgments would not be complete without mentioning my daughter, Eva, and my wife, Suzanne.

— *iii* —

Note the lack of an "e" between the "g" and the "m" in Acknowledgments.

Acknowledgments

Here, the author thanks people who helped write or inspire the work.

Acknowledgments can follow the Dedication or appear in the Back Matter (which is my preference). In old movies, the credits rolled *before* the action started. This worked for captive audiences in theaters, but videotape empowered viewers to hit fast-forward and bypass the opening clutter. Today, the credits come at the *end* of the movie. And some viewers remain in the theater until the end credits have finished rolling.

Readers often skip opening Acknowledgments because they have not yet developed a *relationship* with you or your content. Readers are more likely to read your Acknowledgments at the *back* of your book because you'll have given them a reason to be curious about who helped inspire your story or facilitate your writing process.

The Anatomy of Book Design

Dave Bricker

Colophon

The text of *THE BLUE MONK* is set in Centaur, a refinement of Roman inscriptional capitals designed by Bruce Rogers as a titling design for signage in the Metropolitan Museum. Rogers later designed a lowercase based on Nicolas Jenson's work from the mid-1460s, turning the titling into a full typeface.

The book's title and section headers are set in Old Standard, a digital revival by Alexey Kryukov of a serif typeface commonly used in the late 19th and early 20th century, but almost completely abandoned later.

The corner ornament was selected from Lanston Typeface Corporation's Keystone Ornaments, a set of glyphs based on "running border" ornaments from the Keystone Type foundry of Philadelphia, circa 1903.

The titles on the chart illustrations and the Essential Absurdities Logotype are set in Behrens Antiqua, designed by Peter Behrens in 1902 as a corporate typeface to emulate hand-rendered display lettering while maintaining consistency across artists and applications.

The book's margins are based on the Van de Graaf canon.

Colophon from my book, *The Blue Monk,* 2014.

Colophon

If you're writing a book (and reading this one), you're finding out how much hidden detail goes into producing a published volume. A Colophon allows you to document design decisions—font choices, layout styles, design influences, et cetera—that lie behind the book's interior and exterior aesthetics. A Colophon establishes that you engaged in a *conscious* design process, and thus distinguishes you from the many authors who dump their text into a template or use whatever default font opens up when they create a new word processor document.

Non-designers will likely find this materal to be of little interest. Include a Colophon if your design process produces a book that varies in appearance from a common trade-published book.

Sign-off

You won't find the Sign-off page in other book design or writing references, but it offers a simple and effective way to amplify the marketing power of a book. On the last page of your book, thank your reader and ask them to post a review of your book.

Asking for an *authentic* review conveys that you're looking to succeed on your own merits (As opposed to asking everyone to give you a 5-star rating). It establishes that you are grateful to your reader (which you should be) and that you value their feedback.

From a marketing standpoint, this request serves as a call to action. Readers are more likely to post a review if you *ask* them to.

If you want the reader to contact you—with questions or business inquiries—sign off with your name and contact information. If not, skip this page and consider your book finished.

Questions? Corrections?

If you find an error in this book or don't understand an explanation, that means I failed you. Please let me know so I can fix the problem and put things right.

Email: dave@davebricker.com.

Comments? Opinions?

If you found this book worthy of commentary, please post an authentic review on Amazon.com that explains why you found it valuable (or not).

Example Sign-off created for this book.

Final Page

Leave the final page of your book—the one that faces the inside of the back cover—blank.

Inside Back Cover

In books produced through contemporary mass production this "page" is traditionally left blank; the book binding process ususally requires it to be so, though so some printers do offer "duplex" paperback covers.

In traditional books, the inside front and back cover pages are pasted onto boards that make a book "hard cover."

Antique books were often bound with fanciful "end papers" as depicted in this example.

Outside Back Cover

Traditional back covers were either left blank or offered "wraparound" elements that continued the front cover design.

Paperbacks and mass marketing changed all that. Today's back cover usually displays a bar-code, and publishers have other design decisions to make:

If your book will be physically held by a prospective reader while being evaluated for purchase, the inclusion of a description, endorsements, a brief professional author bio, an excerpt, and/or some highlighted "takeaway points" can help you close a sale.

If your book will only be sold online, consider omitting the commercial verbiage. There's plenty of room for that on your website and on your book's bookstore page. Instead of writing marketing copy that will never be read, consider the value of a simple, elegant design. Sometimes this is as easy to accomplish as wrapping the front cover image around the spine to the back.

See this book's back cover for an example of a "commercial" approach.